To

From

Date

Published by Barbour Publishing, Inc., P.O. Box 719, Uhrichsville, Ohio 44683, www.barbourbooks.com

*Our mission is to publish and distribute inspirational products offering exceptional value and biblical encouragement to the masses.*

 Member of the
Evangelical Christian
Publishers Association

Printed in Malaysia.

# THINKING OF You

BARBOUR
PUBLISHING

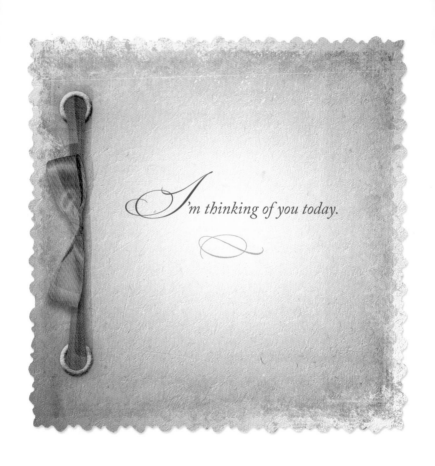

*I'm thinking of you today.*

*If I had a single flower for every time
I thought about you, I could
walk forever in my garden.*

CLAUDIA GHANDI

*God gave us memories that we might
have roses in December.*

JAMES M. BARRIE

*I'm thinking of you today. . .*
*and wishing you sunshine.*

*I thank my God every time I remember you.*

PHILIPPIANS 1:3 NIV

*There is no event so commonplace*
*but that God is present within it. . .*
*always leaving you room to recognize*
*Him or not recognize Him.*

FREDERICK BUECHNER

*Never lose an opportunity of seeing anything
that is beautiful, for beauty is God's handwriting—
a wayside sacrament. Welcome it in every fair face,
in every fair sky, in every fair flower, and thank
God for it as a cup of blessing.*

RALPH WALDO EMERSON

*Expect a surprise every day!*

*A thing of beauty is a joy forever;
its loveliness increases.*

JOHN KEATS

*I'm thinking of you today. . .and wishing you
the knowledge of God's presence.*

*God. . .is everywhere present.*

ARTHUR FOOTE

*Never forget that you are not alone.
God is with you, helping and guiding.
He is the companion who never fails,
the friend whose love comforts and strengthens.
Have faith, and He will do everything for you.*

AUROBINDO

*Each new day that comes your way*
*is blessed with promise.*

*Keep love in your heart. A life without it is*
*like a sunless garden when the flowers are dead.*
*The consciousness of loving and being loved*
*bring a warmth and richness to life*
*that nothing else can bring.*

Oscar Wilde

*May love shine down on you always.*

*When you are down, I wish you joy.*

*Where your pleasure is, there is your treasure;*
*where your treasure, there your heart;*
*where your heart, there your happiness.*

AUGUSTINE OF HIPPO

*Nothing is worth more than this day.*

JOHANN WOLFGANG VON GOETHE

*Trust God from the bottom
of your heart.*

*You can trust God right
now to supply all
your needs for today.
And if your needs are more
tomorrow, His supply will
be greater also.*

*Live today fully, expressing gratitude
for all you have been, all you are right now,
and all you are becoming.*

MELODIE BEATTIE

*Happiness consists more in small
conveniences or pleasures that occur every day,
than in great pieces of good fortune that happen
but seldom to a man in the course of his life.*

BENJAMIN FRANKLIN

*The spirit of happiness is a sheer miracle.
It is the gift of the happy God.*

AMY CARMICHAEL

*May gentle and beautiful
moments be yours today.*

*The sun does not shine for a few trees
and flowers, but for the wide world's joy.*

HENRY WARD BEECHER

*Enjoy the
little things, for one
day you may look back
and realize they were
the big things.*

ROBERT BRAULT

*When you are troubled, I wish you peace.*

*The best and most beautiful things in the world
cannot be seen or even touched.
They must be felt with the heart.*

HELEN KELLER

*Take time today for quiet moments
of reflection.*

*Isn't everything you have
and everything you are sheer gifts from God?*

1 Corinthians 4:7 msg

*I am beginning to learn that it is the sweet,
simple things of life which are the real ones after all.*

Laura Ingalls Wilder

*Little deeds of kindness, little words of love,
help to make earth happy, like the heaven above.*

Julie A. Fletcher Carney

*Dear Jesus, give me
a child's heart that sees the lovely,
simple things in life.
Amen.*

*Look for the good in everything
and everyone, and you will find it.*

*Cheerfulness is the offshoot of goodness.*

CHRISTIAN NESTELL BOVEE

*Every heart that has beat strong and cheerfully*
*has left a hopeful impulse behind it in the world*
*and bettered the tradition of mankind.*

ROBERT LOUIS STEVENSON

*Cheerfulness brings sunshine to the soul and*
*drives away the shadows of anxiety.*

HANNAH WHITALL SMITH

*We look at our burdens and heavy loads*
*and shrink from them; but as we lift them*
*and bind them about our hearts, they become wings,*
*and on them we rise and soar toward God.*

MRS. CHARLES E. COWMAN

*We may run, walk, stumble. . .or fly,*
*but let us never lose sight of the reason*
*for the journey or miss a chance to see*
*a rainbow on the way.*

GLORIA GAITHER

*Have you ever come on anything quite like
this extravagant generosity of God. . . ?*

Romans 11:33 MSG

*Dear Lord, thank You for the gifts
of love, comfort, laughter. . .
and countless blessings. Amen.*

*May the sun always shine
on your windowpane; may the hand of
a friend always be near you; may God fill
your heart with gladness to cheer you.*

IRISH BLESSING

*The best things in life are never rationed.
Friendship, loyalty, love do not require coupons.*

GEORGE T. HEWITT

*The greatest healing therapy is
friendship and love.*

HUBERT HUMPHREY

*The more we love, the better we are.*

JEREMY TAYLOR

*The lives that have been the greatest*
*blessing to you are the lives of*
*those people who themselves were unaware*
*of having been a blessing.*

OSWALD CHAMBERS

*It is a comely fashion to be glad—*
*joy is the grace we say to God.*

JEAN INGELOW

❧

*Laugh and be well.*

MATTHEW GREEN

❧

*Happiness is something to do,*
*something to love, something to hope for.*

CHINESE PROVERB

*It is astonishing
how short a time it takes
for very wonderful
things to happen.*

Frances Hodgson Burnett

*Love conquers all things.*

VIRGIL

*We can share with each other
without being threatened by
each other's differences because we know
that we are united by Christ,
and this union is a union of love.*

MADELEINE L'ENGLE

*He who sows courtesy reaps friendship,
and he who plants kindness gathers love.*

SAINT BASIL

*Love each other with genuine affection,
and take delight in honoring each other.*

ROMANS 12:10 NLT

*Love is all we have, the only way that
each can help the other.*

EURIPIDES

The unselfish effort to bring cheer
to others will be the beginning of a
happier life for ourselves.

HELEN KELLER

*I*t is astonishing how little one
feels alone when one loves.

JOHN BULWER

Human love and the delights of friendship,
out of which are built the memories that endure,
are also to be treasured up as hints
of what shall be hereafter.

BEDE JARRETT

*Every experience God gives us,*
*every person He puts into our lives*
*is the perfect preparation for the future*
*that only He can see.*

CORRIE TEN BOOM

*Dear Father, thank You for watching over me,*
*for meeting all my needs. Amen.*

*God's in His heaven—all's right with the world!*

ROBERT BROWNING

*A person should hear a little music,
read a little poetry, and see a fine picture
every day of their life, in order that worldly
cares may not obliterate the sense of
the beautiful which God has implanted
in the human soul.*

JOHANN WOLFGANG VON GOETHE

*Happiness is a habit; cultivate it.*

ELBERT HUBBARD

*To be alive, to be able to see, to walk,
to have a home. . .it's all a miracle.*

ARTHUR RUBINSTEIN

*Whatsoever is lovely. . .*

*think about such things.*

PHILIPPIANS 4:8 NIV

⧂

*Let me be joy! Be hope! Let my life sing!*

MARY CAROLYN DAVIES

⧂

*One word frees us of all the weight*

*and pain in life. That word is* love.

SOPHOCLES

*True happiness comes when we stop
complaining about all the troubles
we have and offer thanks for all the
troubles we don't have.*

UNKNOWN

*Whoever is happy will make others happy, too.*

ANNE FRANK

*Stretch out your hand and take
the world's wide gifts of joy and beauty.*

CORRINE ROOSEVELT ROBINSON

*When things are complicated,*
*I wish you simple beauty.*

*All things bright and beautiful,*
*All creatures great and small,*
*All things wise and wonderful,*
*The Lord God made them all.*

CECIL FRANCES ALEXANDER

*True wisdom lies in gathering the precious*
*things out of each day as it goes by.*

E. S. BOUTON

*If you keep a smile tucked away*
*in your heart, it's easy to keep one on your face.*

UNKNOWN

*One filled with joy preaches without preaching.*

MOTHER TERESA

*I think I began learning long ago
that those who are happiest are those who
do the most for others.*

BOOKER T. WASHINGTON

❦

*The best exercise for strengthening the heart is
reaching down and lifting people up.*

ERNEST BLEVINS

❦

*The true source of cheerfulness
is benevolence. The soul that perpetually
overflows with kindness and sympathy
will always be cheerful.*

PARKE GODWIN

*Being confident of this very thing,
that he which hath begun a good work in you
will perform it until the day of Jesus Christ.*

PHILIPPIANS 1:6 KJV

*Life is God's novel. Let Him write it.*

ISAAC SINGER

*The less I pray, the harder it gets;*
*the more I pray, the better it goes.*

MARTIN LUTHER

*Daily prayers lessen daily cares.*

UNKNOWN

*God's arms of love are around you,*
*and He is only a prayer away.*

*Every man prays in his own language, and there is no language that God does not understand.*

DUKE ELLINGTON

*rue prayer is not to be found in the words of the mouth but in the thoughts of the heart.*

GREGORY THE GREAT

*I have held many things in my hands
and I have lost them all; but whatever
I have placed in God's hands, that I still possess.*

MARTIN LUTHER

*Gladly accept the gifts of the present hour.*

HORACE

*Every minute should be enjoyed and savored.*

EARL NIGHTINGALE

*Have confidence in God's mercy,*
*for when you think He is a long way from you,*
*He is often quite near.*

Thomas à Kempis

*Taste the small blessings God sprinkles through your days.*

Dear friend, I pray that you may enjoy good health and that all may go well with you.

3 JOHN 1:2 NIV

*Be on the lookout for mercies. The more we look for them, the more of them we will see.*

MALTBIE D. BABCOCK

*I'm thinking of you today. . .*
*and wishing you a day filled with delight.*

*Let us be grateful to people who*
*make us happy; they are the charming*
*gardeners who make our souls blossom.*

Marcel Proust

*Joy is the net of love by which you can catch souls.*

Mother Teresa

*Open your heart to God's joy!*

*Always laugh when you can.*

LORD BYRON

*Mirth is God's medicine.*
*Everybody ought to bathe in it.*

HENRY WARD BEECHER

*May your life be full of
God's joyful surprises!*

*Life is a splendid gift—there is
nothing small about it.*

FLORENCE NIGHTINGALE

*Into* all lives, in many simple, familiar, homely ways, God infuses this element of joy from the surprises of life, which unexpectedly brighten our days and fill our eyes with light.

HENRY WADSWORTH LONGFELLOW

*You are in God's hands.*

*What happens when we live God's way?*
*He brings gifts into our lives, much the same*
*way that fruit appears in an orchard.*

GALATIANS 5:22 MSG

*Add to your joy by counting your blessings.*

UNKNOWN

*Try not to be so busy that you miss the many*
*small gifts that God's offering you today.*
*Take the time to enjoy life. Each moment is*
*a tiny treasure, filled with new blessings*
*from the God who loves you.*

*If you surrender completely to the moments*
*as they pass, you live more richly those moments.*

ANNE MORROW LINDBERGH

*God is at work in ways you cannot see. Trust Him.*

*Love is an image of God, and not a lifeless
image but the living essence of the divine
nature which means full of all goodness.*

MARTIN LUTHER

*The supreme happiness of life is in the
conviction that we are loved; loved for ourselves,
or rather, in spite of ourselves.*

VICTOR HUGO

*Remember that God will always love you—no matter what!*

*I'm praying that today, as you go about your routine, you'll sense God's quiet love in all you do, in all those you meet, and in every breath you take.*

*Keep your face upturned to [God] as the flowers do the sun. Look, and your soul shall live and grow.*

HANNAH WHITALL SMITH

*Wake each morning with a sense of hope.*
*God has amazing things in store for you.*
*And He does all things well.*

❧

*God puts each fresh morning, each new chance*
*of life into our hands as a gift to see what*
*we will do with it.*

UNKNOWN

❧

*A new life begins for us with every second.*
*Let us go forward joyously to meet it.*
*We must press on, whether we will or no,*
*and we shall walk better with our eyes before us*
*than with them ever behind.*

JEROME K. JEROME

*When things seem empty, I wish you abundant life.*

*"For I know the plans I have for you,"*
*declares the LORD, "plans to prosper you and not to*
*harm you, plans to give you hope and a future."*

JEREMIAH 29:11 NIV

*Spend time each day conversing with God.*
*He'll bless you for it.*

*God always gives His best to those*
*who leave the choice with Him.*

JIM ELLIOT

*Happy is he who yields himself*
*completely. . .to God.*

FRANÇOIS FENELON

*Go to sleep in peace. God is awake.*

VICTOR HUGO

*I wish you all the joy that you can wish.*

WILLIAM SHAKESPEARE

*The happiness of life is made up of
minute fractions—the little soon-forgotten
charities of a kiss or a smile, a kind look or
heartfelt compliment.*

SAMUEL TAYLOR COLERIDGE

*What do we live for, if it is not to make
life less difficult for each other?*

GEORGE ELIOT

*The greatest gift we can give
one another is rapt attention to
one another's existence.*

SUE ATCHLEY EBAUGH

*That I am here is a wonderful mystery*

*to which I will respond with joy.*

UNKNOWN

*God's most wonderful creation is you!*

*You are here to enrich the world.*

WOODROW WILSON

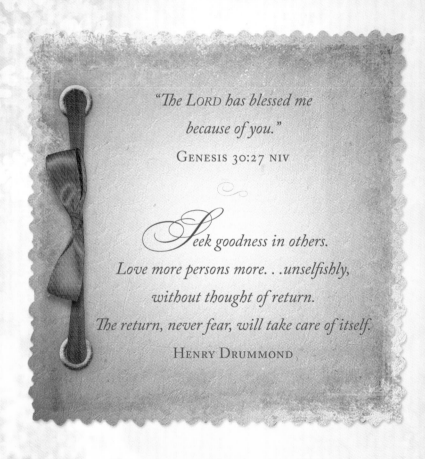

"The LORD has blessed me
because of you."

GENESIS 30:27 NIV

*Seek goodness in others.
Love more persons more. . .unselfishly,
without thought of return.
The return, never fear, will take care of itself.*

HENRY DRUMMOND

*I'm praying that you'll see
the reality of God's promises.*

❧

*God's promises are like the stars.*

DAVID NICHOLAS

*Life is what we are alive to.
It is not length but breadth. . . .
Be alive to. . .goodness, kindness, purity,
love, history, poetry, music, flowers,
stars, God, and eternal hope.*

MALTBIE D. BABCOCK

*May you see the angels' hands
at work in your life!*

*All God's angels come to us disguised.*

JAMES RUSSELL LOWELL

*The art of life is to live in the present
moment and to make that moment as perfect
as we can by the realization that we are
the instruments and expression of God Himself.*

EMMET FOX

*The secret to enjoying life is to be thankful*
*for what each day brings.*

*Write it on your heart that every day*
*is the best day of the year.*

RALPH WALDO EMERSON

*Human beings ought to. . .*
*share all the gifts they have received from God.*

MEISTER ECKHART

*The most precious things in life are near at hand.*

JOHN BURROUGHS

*In your daily routine, in the stressful
details of ordinary life, when you least
expect it, may grace leap out at you,
encouraging your heart.*

*And we know that in all things God works*
*for the good of those who love him.*

ROMANS 8:28 NIV

❧

*I'm praying that your life will be*
*lit with flashes of grace.*

*Don't get so busy that you forget to simply be.*
*Sometimes the best way to stop being*
*overwhelmed by life is to simply step back,*
*take a day. . .or an hour. . .or a moment,*
*and notice all that God is doing in your life.*

*Fill up the crevices of time*
*with the things that matter most.*

AMY CARMICHAEL

*When we take time to notice
the simple things in life, we never lack
for encouragement. We discover we are
surrounded by limitless hope that's just
wearing everyday clothes.*

UNKNOWN

*Every day holds the possibility
of a miracle.*

*Be cheerful no matter what;*
*pray all the time; thank God no matter*
*what happens. This is the way God wants*
*you who belong to Christ Jesus to live.*

1 THESSALONIANS 5:16–18 MSG